Meals Ahoy!

GOURMET
MEALS
ON YOUR BOAT

CHEF KELLY

Library of Congress Control Number: 2011912474

ISBN: Softcover   978-1-4628-9773-5
         Hardcover   978-1-4628-9774-2

To order additional copies of this book, contact:
Xlibris Corporation
1-888-795-4274
www.Xlibris.com
Orders@Xlibris.com

This book was printed in the United States of America.

As a child, I watched my dear mother cook with her soul and spirit, never using a measuring device and seldom tasting her cooking, which always turned out to be so wonderful. I always wondered about her secret to such delicious food and was determined at an early age to spend as much time as possible in the kitchen to learn how she mesmerized our taste buds.

From my early days in the Caribbean to my adult life in the U.S. and Canada to travels abroad, I have continually been inspired to prepare wonderful meals people could enjoy. I have picked up recipes from quaint little bistros in the cobblestone streets of Paris and Rome, the pensions of Florence, haute cuisine of London and Geneva, venues on the Adriatic Coast as well as my roots in the Caribbean. And through all of this inspiration I've had the unique opportunity to travel the globe as a gourmet chef leaving my culinary stamp with satisfied gourmet enthusiasts everywhere.

I opened my first restaurant in my teens and went on to own seven more over the years. Cooking is my life and my approach to excellent food is to create a culinary experience that will tantalize your taste buds that exceed expectations.

Designing a cookbook especially for boaters has allowed me to combine my passions for cooking and boating. From excursions in the Pacific Northwest, sailing across the South Pacific, exploring the Great Lakes, traversing the Bermuda Triangle, to numerous trips in the Caribbean, I've not only been a sailor but the cook as well. All of those hours in the galley have paid off with unique expertise that I am excited to share with you in this book.

Cooking on a boat can be as easy as cooking at home. The key to successful boat meals is provisioning – you must prepare ahead! If you provision with junk food, you will eat junk food. But if you provision with gourmet ingredients, you will eat gourmet meals.

Entertaining on a boat is also quite easy. In this book I will share my years of experience in the galley to help you create simple, easy meals that will wow and impress. Each recipe quickly takes the stress out of entertaining and actually makes it fun.

Every recipe has been tested numerous times – not in a test kitchen, but in a boat galley. You will find that the recipes are simple and can be made even easier by doing some quick prep work before boarding.

For those who fish while boating, some of the most memorable meals are those made from the catch of the day. To help you savor those special occasions, there is an extensive set of fish recipes. Of course they can also be used with fish already on board.

I hope you will love and cherish this cookbook as much as I do. Make sure to keep a copy at home for provisioning and one on the boat for cooking. And the next time you head out on a boating trip you will have the confidence to go gourmet. Meals ahoy!

- Chef Kelly

RULES OF PROVISIONING

1. Get yourself a heavy plastic apron. Spills on a boat are common, and a cloth apron will absorb hot liquids, and your belly will pay. Believe me, I know. While crossing the South Pacific, we were in twenty-five-foot waves for sixteen hours, and I cooked every meal; and if I did not have a plastic apron, getting burned at the equator on a forty-five-foot sailboat would be no fun.

2. A refrigerator is great but not necessary. An icebox or cooler is a good idea. However, if you are doing blue-water sailing, those luxuries are not always available. So you must stow dry foods, canned foods, and dehydrated foods. If you are enjoying daily or weekly boating, fresh foods are the best.

3. You must be prepared. Try and obtain all the ingredients in your recipe before you cast off. That means that you must read your recipes beforehand. On the ocean or the lake, you cannot just run to the corner store. You must be able to substitute items and spices in your recipes.

4. If you do not take extended trips, try to keep your spices in plastic freezer bags. For long trips, use small Tupperware plastic containers as spices will last longer and stay fresher. Try to stay away from glass bottles for anything. They can break and pose danger and are much heavier especially if you are a racer.

5. Take the food that you know you will enjoy, and lots of it. Not things you think you may need. Plan your meals. Two or three meals a day and snacks. Whatever number of meals per day you may need, plan it so you can shop right. Planning your meals is also important because you can pre-prepare certain menus that will make your life easier on the water.

6. If you are lucky enough to have refrigeration or an ice box, package all frozen foods properly, preferably in freezer bags. Frozen foods should be used first then your dry or canned foods. This is why daily menu and food planning is very important. On my trip from Tahiti to Hawaii a few years ago, our fridge gave up the ghost. We had to use all our fresh and frozen products quickly, which was a waste—the lesson here is you know what I mean. Use refrigerated food first on long trips. However, if you are just on a weekend boating trip, you will not have a major problem. Remember, take enough ice with you on your short trips even though you have refrigeration.

7. Every item, tool or whatever you keep on a boat must have a home. That is where it lives. The reason for this is that in an emergency, you do not have to try and locate it. You just go to its home and get it. That includes can or bottle opener, your knives, and all your tools. For this reason I try to purchase wines with twist tops (these could be very good wines), beers also with twist tops, so if you can't find an opener, no problem.

8. Potatoes, onions, and the fruits you bring aboard will have a shortened life span if they are left in plastic bags. Try to place them somewhere safe to prevent them from going bad. My boat had a dry bilge, so I had a container there for storage.

DON'T LEAVE LAND WITHOUT IT

Some of these items I refer to as "take with" items. They should be on your boat when you are on the boat.

1. PFDs, your emergency kit, flares, first aid kit, tools, paper charts, etc.
2. Your menu ingredients
3. Chopping knives
4. Dining knives and forks
5. Boat china (unbreakable mugs, bowls, and plates, etc.)
6. Can and bottle opener
7. Matches and lighter
8. Stainless steel mixing bowls
9. Thermo carafe
10. Potato peeler
11. Stainless steel mini grates
12. Expresso mixer (optional)
13. Coffee mugs with base grip
14. Freezer bags
15. Mini garbage bags
16. Thermos
17. Plastic storage containers, rubber made
18. Towels (paper and cloth)
19. Plastic apron
20. Cockpit knife or hatchet
21. Waterproof flashlight
22. Extra line
23. Collapsible measuring colander
24. Potato masher
25. Pots and pans (large enough to hold food for at least four, sauce pans, etc)
26. Dried fruits and any other snacks
27. Rain gear
28. Cleaning products
29. Garbage bags
30. You must file a trip plan with the coast guard and family members, which should include arrival dates and return dates.

MEALS AHOY!
BE PREPARED BEFORE YOU CAST OFF

APPETIZERS AND VEGETARIAN

SALADS

FISH

MEAT

CHICKEN

PASTA

SANDWICHES, SOUPS and BREAKFAST

SIDES, PASTAS AND VEGGIES

Appetizers and Vegetarian

Stuffed Mushrooms

INGREDIENTS:

12 large mushrooms, cleaned and stems removed and chopped

1 cup baby shrimp, chopped (crab meat, imitation crab, or any fish of your choice)

4 slices of pancetta or bacon, minced (optional)

4–6 sprigs of parsley or cilantro, finely minced

2 garlic cloves, minced or pressed

½ medium onions, finely minced

1 cup fine bread crumbs

1 egg, beaten

3 tbsp olive oil for sautéing

½ tsp of dry oregano

½ tsp (2.5 g) of dry marjoram

½ cup crumbled feta or cheese of your choice

salt and pepper

METHOD:

Heat oil in a frying pan. When hot, add onions and garlic and sauté until onions are translucent about 3–5 minutes. Do not burn. Turn heat down and add pancetta, mushroom stems, and shrimp. Sauté for another 5 minutes. Add bread crumbs, oregano, and marjoram. Mix, making sure that all ingredients are combined. Turn the heat off and add the cheese and egg and mix some more. Add parsley, salt and pepper to taste.

To stuff mushrooms: Using a spoon, scoop up some mixture and fill mushroom caps (about 1 tablespoon). In the meantime, heat oven to 375°. When all caps are filled, place them on a baking sheet and bake for 20 minutes. Remove from oven, place on serving platter, drizzle with olive oil, garnish with parsley, and serve hot or at room temperature.

Note: The pancetta is salty, so adjust carefully with salt. If mixture is too dry and does not hold together in a spoon, add a little water. The mushrooms will stay upright if baked in a muffin pan.

Pacific Sushi

METHOD:

This recipe requires that you freeze the fish before preparation. Remove the fish from the freezer. Thaw the fish just enough until it is still firm. Slice into thin strips. Place into a dish. Add all ingredients except the bacon. Mix well and refrigerate for at least 3 hours. Overnight is better.

To serve, place slices on a piece of bread, sprinkle with chopped onion and bacon, and garnish with a sprig of parsley.

Note: If salmon is used, do not add lemon to marinade as this will discolor the fish. Add just before serving. However if you prefer to use cooked fish, steam the fish first, then proceed to add other ingredients.

INGREDIENTS:

8 slices of baguette, cut at an angle about ½ inch thick

1 lb fresh bonito fillet or wild salmon, thinly sliced

6 strips of bacon, fried and crumbled

8 tablespoons of dry wasabi mixed with water or store-bought prepared wasabi

1 tbsp sweet white wine vinegar

1 tbsp finely chopped red or yellow onions. Save some for garnishing.

juice of 1 lemon

1 tbsp capers chopped

3 tbsp virgin olive oil

1 tsp sea salt

1 tbsp chopped dill

3 tbsp chopped chives

Akara (Fish Fritters)

Just about any fish fillet can be used in this recipe. Sailing in the tropics, salted cod (bacalao) is commonly used. This can also be found in most ethnic or large chain grocery stores. Crab meat, poached salmon, tilapia, or even poached fresh cod is also used. If salted cod is used, the salt must be removed. This can be done by either soaking the cod overnight and changing the water at least twice or by boiling the cod and changing the water at least once.

INGREDIENTS:

1 lb poached fresh fish or salted cod (salt removed)

1 cup flour

1 ½ cups of water

2 tbsp baking powder

1 tbsp curry powder

½ medium onion, finely chopped

3 garlic cloves, finely chopped

1 head of green onions, finely chopped

4–6 sprigs chopped cilantro, Italian parsley can be used

cooking oil for frying

½ small jalapeño (optional)

1 tbsp salt to taste

Dipping sauce for akara:

3 tbsp. mayonaise

2 tbsp. sweet chilli sauce or any other sauce

1 tbsp. dijon mustard or plain mustard

Few flakes of hot pepper

Mix all and use to dip fish cakes.

METHOD:

Poach the fish, drain off water, and let it cool. Crush the fish with your hands or with a fork. Add all the dry ingredients to fish and combine thoroughly. Add water a little at a time until a soft dough is formed, which can be lifted with a spoon. If mixture is too dry, more water can be added.

Heat oil on medium heat. Add one tablespoon of mixture to frying pan at a time. Continue to add more mixture to hot oil. Do not overcrowd the frying pan. When the cakes are brown on one side, turn them over to cook the other side. Remove the cakes from frying pan and place on a paper towel to absorb oil. Continue to fry cakes till the mixture is used up. To serve, place fish cakes on a platter. Garnish with lemon slices and a sprig of parsley, and serve at room temperature.

Tent Island Mussels

(STUFFED MUSSELS ON THE HALF SHELL)

INGREDIENTS:

12 shelled mussels, cleaned and keep half of the shells for serving

2 tbsp butter

2 tbsp olive oil

1 cup milk

½ cup white wine

2 tbsp flour

½ medium red onion, finely chopped

2 eggs beaten

1 cup of fine bread crumbs

METHOD:

Melt butter in VOO (virgin olive oil) and fry onions. Do not burn. Add flour and make rue. Add wine and slowly bring to a boil. Slowly add milk while mixing. If too thick, add more milk till a sauce consistency is achieved. Season with salt and pepper to taste. Add mussels and cook for another 5 minutes. Stuff half shells with mussels, place on a serving plate, and pour sauce over mussels. Serve and garnish with lemon wedges and parsley.

Alternatively, the mussels can be removed from the sauce, rolled in an egg mixture, then bread crumbs, and placed on the half shell, then bake in the oven at 375° for 10 minutes or until brown.

Annette Inlet Prawns

(PRAWNS IN GARLIC SAUCE)

INGREDIENTS:

1 lb large headless and deveined prawns with tails attached

4 garlic cloves, chopped

½ chili or ½ tsp pepper flakes, pepper seeds removed and chopped (optional)

½ cup virgin olive oil

½ baguette sliced

cilantro or Italian parsley for garnishing

¼ cup sweet white wine

juice of ½ piece of lemon and lemon wedges to garnish

parsley to garnish

METHOD:

Heat oil in a frying pan and sauté garlic for 2 minutes. Be careful not to burn. Add prawns and cook for another 3 minutes while mixing. And wine and reduce for another 3 minutes. Add lemon juice and mix.

Garnish with lemon wedges and parsley, and serve with bread slices.

Abaco Prawns
(BATTERED PRAWNS)

This recipe is done in two stages. The prawns are poached, then dipped in a batter and fried.

1 lb prawns (20–30 count)
8 cups of water
2 tbsp salt
juice of 1 lemon
½ cup of white wine

Bring the water to a boil. Add the salt and the juice of the lemon and boil for 3 minutes. Remove the prawns immediately, and let it cool.

BATTER:
1 cup flour
2 eggs
3 tbsp milk
2 tbsp oil
1 tsp salt
oil for frying

Mix all ingredients. If batter is too watery, add some more flour. Dip prawns in batter, and fry in hot oil. Careful not to crowd the frying pan or burn prawns. Turn prawns once one side is brown, remove from frying pan, and place on paper towel. To serve, place prawns on a platter and garnish with lemon slices. This dish can also be served as a main course over rice or pasta.

Note: Panko and an egg wash can be use to bread prawns instead of making the batter.

Chicken of the Sea
(SEARED SCALLOPS ON CRISPY WONTONS)

INGREDIENTS:
1 tsp salt
¼ cup VOO
12 large sea scallops marinated in salt and VOO
2 tbsp butter
rind of one lemon
2 garlic cloves
1 sprig of green onion
unsalted butter for sautéing
12 store-bought wontons, cut into 2-inch circles and pan fried till golden brown and crispy. Set aside on absorbent paper.

METHOD:

Sauté garlic and lemon rind. Sprinkle scallop with salt and pepper and cook for 2 minute each side. Place green onion on each wonton, top with scallop. Spoon over juices left in pan over scallop, garnish with lemon slices and Italian parsley, and serve.

Drunken Shrimp

Prawns and tequila are married in this recipe. I developed this recipe while sailing on the Sea of Cortez. My friend, whose boat we were sailing to Mexico, could only cook macaroni and cheese. He added prawns and had tequila as a beverage. What a disaster. So this recipe was born.

INGREDIENTS:
1 lb prawns 20–30 count

¼ cup tequila

4 cloves of garlic

½ tsp paprika

1 tbsp herbes de Provence (1 tsp dry marjoram, 1 tsp dry oregano)

¼ cup VOO for sautéing

1 tbsp salt

½ juice of a lemon

¼ cup cilantro

4 sprigs of cilantro, chopped

METHOD:

Sauté garlic in oil. Add the prawns and cook for another 2 minutes. Add the tequila and sauté for another 2 minutes. Add lemon juice, herbes de Provence, and paprika. Adjust with salt and pepper, add cilantro, toss and arrange on platter.

Vegetarian Dip
ROASTED EGGPLANT DIP (BABA GHANOUSH)

This appetizer can be started at home and completed on the boat. However, if you have a grill or oven on board, this is simple.

INGREDIENTS:

2 medium eggplants, peeled and thinly sliced

4 tbsp VOO

1 head of garlic

4 sprigs of fresh basil, finely chopped

1 tsp cumin

3 toasted pita (grilled or pan fried), cut in triangles.

METHOD:

In an oven heated at 375°, roast eggplants for at least ¾ hour. When done, let it cool. At the same time, chop head off the garlic, fill with VOO, wrap in tinfoil, and bake for 45 minutes. Cool garlic and squeeze cloves out. Puree or crush meat of eggplants and garlic. Serve with toasted pita or chips.

Cabo Tequila Avocado

INGREDIENTS:

1 pineapple, peeled and sliced horizontally and soaked in tequila

1 cup tequila

3–4 ripe avocados crushed

juice from 2 limes

8 oz of whipped cream

METHOD:

Blend or mix lime juice and avocados, and fold in whipped cream. In the meantime, grill or broil pineapple slices. Top with avocado mix and serve.

Salads

Not~Too~Spicy Potato Salad

We had some potatoes, tomato sauce, chili peppers, olive oil, and onion. Yes, we were close to the equator out in the deep blue sea, and one member of the crew had the urge for potato salad, and all of a sudden, we all did. All eyes focused on me, so down to the galley I went. The above ingredients are all I could find. Not even a teaspoon of mayo. The following was my concoction.

If using new potatoes, do not peel. Cut potatoes in half or quarters depending on the size. Parboil, drain, and set aside. Sauté chili peppers and onions in oil and add to boiled potatoes. Mix well. Pour some canned tomato sauce over potatoes. Do not add too much sauce, just enough to coat. Adjust with salt and pepper. You may add any other herb, such as Italian parsley and cilantro. Serve on large platter.

There are no measurements in this recipe. The amount of salad will depend on the number of guests. Also you can use mayo instead of tomato sauce if it is available.

Trini Salad

The island of Trinidad and Tobago in the West Indies is famous for its authentic foods. Boating in the Caribbean is an experience by itself. Cooking fresh food from the market is exhilarating. While shopping, just let your imagination flow. This salad got its name from the short version of the natives.

INGREDIENTS:

3 ripe tomatoes sliced horizontally ¼ inch thick

1 English or 2 regular cucumbers cubed. Do not remove the seeds.

1 yellow zucchini

1 red pepper, diced

1 head of green onions cut into quarter inch lengths, making sure to include the white section of the onion

2 sprigs each of Italian parsley and cilantro chopped

juice of 1 lemon

4 tbsp olive oil

a pinch of white sugar

salt and pepper to taste

For dressing, mix lemon juice, oil, and sugar. Combine all other ingredients with the dressing, and adjust to taste with salt and freshly ground black pepper. Serve in a bowl.

Roasted Red Pepper and Tuna Salad

This is a simple salad and can be made into a light lunch on a beautiful summer day. All the ingredients can be store-bought and brought on board. Just assemble when you are ready for lunch or dinner.

INGREDIENTS:

6 slices of baguette or chapatti bread

1 bottle of roasted red pepper

1 medium onion, finely chopped

2 cans of tuna, about 8 ounces

¼ cup of olive oil

2 tbsp of finely chopped dill

1 tbsp of capers, chopped

METHOD:

Cut peppers lengthwise. Sauté onions in oil until translucent. Add peppers and capers, and fry lightly. Remove from frying pan and set aside. Warm tuna in frying pan and add dill. Do not crush too much. To build tuna salad, top bread slices with pepper and onion mix then some tuna on top. Garnish with dill.

Smoked salmon can also be used. Remember that the capers and fish used may have sufficient salt. Otherwise adjust with salt. Also instead of bread, any form of lettuce can be used. In this case, chop leaves roughly and add to fish and pepper mix.

Pacific Seafood Salad

INGREDIENTS:

2 medium spring onions, sliced about ½ inch

2 sprigs cilantro or parsley, chopped

1 medium onion, sliced

1 lb of headless prawns (30–50 count), peeled

2 lb of mussels, cleaned

½ cup of VOO, save half for dressing

2 tbsp sherry vinegar

¼ cup of white wine

2 tbsp sea salt and 1 tsp salt for dressing

2 cups of water

METHOD:

Bring water, sliced onion, wine, half of the oil, and salt to a boil. Add prawns. Remove from boiling water when they turn pink, and let it cool. Save the water to boil mussels. When mussels open, they are cooked. Remove from boiling water and cool. Once cool, remove the meat. Dissolve 1 tsp salt in sherry and VOO. Add the spring onion, cilantro, prawns, and mussels. Let it rest for at least ½ hour before serving.

Abaco Tuna Salad

While sailing in the Bahamas with two other friends, we decided that we would make use of the best fish we could lay our hands on. Tuna, conch, and any local catch. This recipe can also be made with what ever smoke fish you have on hand.

INGREDIENTS:
1- 8-oz can of tuna chunks
2 roasted red peppers,
store-bought and sliced
2 tomatoes cut into wedges
2 hard-boiled eggs,
roughly chopped
1 cup ripe olives, sliced
juice of 1 lemon
2 tsp dill
½ tsp cumin
salt and pepper
2 sprigs parsley
¼ cup VOO

To make dressing, mix VOO, a little salt, dill, and lemon juice. Mix all other ingredients except the tuna, drizzle with dressing and toss salad. To serve, put tuna in the center of a platter and place the salad around the tuna. Garnish top of the tuna with parsley or dill.

Bahama Squid Salad

INGREDIENTS:

1 lb of squid rings, store-bought

2 tbsp VOO

2 tbsp butter

½ cup yogurt

½ cup cubed mango

2 small zucchini, diced

2 stalks of celery, diced

juice of 1 lemon or lime

1 tbsp Worcestershire sauce

1 tsp smoked hot paprika or regular Hungarian paprika

METHOD:

Sauté squid in oil and butter till tender. Season with salt and refrigerate. Combine remaining ingredients in a bowl. Add squid and refrigerate till ready to use. Serve on bed of lettuce.

Gig Harbor Salad

This classic salad is another easy boat favorite. Sailing through the San Juan and Gulf Islands on the West Coast, this vegetarian dish is healthy, and prep time is quick.

INGREDIENTS:

¼ cup sesame oil

zest from 1 lemon and juice from ½ of a lemon

½ a red onion finely chopped

2 cups of cooked quinoa

1 cup edamame beans, cooked

1 can of black beans

1 tbsp of cumin

2 garlic cloves, finely minced

METHOD:

Use some of the sesame oil to sauté garlic on low heat. Add the cumin and cook for another 1 minute. Add all other ingredients and oil, and cook on low heat while mixing occasionally for 5 more minutes. Remove from heat. Let it cool to room temperature or in refrigerator and serve as a cold salad. This can be served warm as a main course also.

Montague Harbor Japanese Quinoa and Edamame Salad

Now here is a delicious, nutritious and simple salad on a boat. Not time consuming and very satisfying. This makes a very good lunch on a hot summer day.

INGREDIENTS:

2 cups quinoa, cooked
1 cup black beans
2 cups edamame beans cooked
2 tbsp soy sauce
3 tbsp sesame oil
juice of 1 lime

METHOD:

Mix all ingredients thoroughly and serve on lettuce leaf.

West Coast Smoked Salmon Pasta Salad

Talking about boating on the inside passage. Now here is a true northwest salad to celebrate the occasion.

INGREDIENTS:

2 cups of penne or your favorite
pasta cooked al dente
8 oz of smoked salmon
1 cup of frozen peas, thawed
½ cup of mayo
2 tbsp VOO
½ medium red onion, minced
4 sprigs of Italian parsley or
cilantro, chopped
salt and pepper

METHOD:

Cook the pasta in salted water until al dente. Drain and while still hot, add all the other ingredients and combine some more. Can be served hot or refrigerated and served as a salad.

Watermelon and Arugula Salad

INGREDIENTS:

2 cups cubed goat cheese

2 cups cubed fresh watermelon deseeded

1 bunch arugula (1/2 lb.), washed and leafed

4 sprigs (1 cup) roughly chopped mint leaves

juice from one orange

juice from one lemon

1 cup VOO

1 tsp Dijon mustard

1 tsp honey

salt and pepper to taste

DRESSING:

Mix juice from orange and lemon with VOO. Add honey and Dijon, and adjust with salt. Just before serving, toss arugula water melon and all other ingredients with dressing and serve in a bowl.

Quinoa Salad

This is a healthy protein salad. Quinoa is high in protein and is an excellent substitute as a gluten free product.

INGREDIENTS:

2 cups quinoa (1 cup white and 1 cup red can be used. It is prettier.)

water

salt

2 cups frozen mixed vegetables, thawed

1 tbsp cumin

¼ cup VOO

3 garlic cloves, crushed or finely chopped

3 sprigs of cilantro, chopped

METHOD:

Most people will let you believe that it is difficult to cook quinoa, I assure you it is not. If you can cook rice, you can definitely cook quinoa. Boil as much water as you want with salt to taste. Once water is boiling, add a little oil and the quinoa. Now here is the key: Let quinoa boil for 13 minutes. Drain water in colander with small holes. Do not run cold water on quinoa. In the meantime, sauté garlic and cumin and vegetables in frying pan. Remove from heat and add quinoa. Add cilantro and some more VOO if you wish. Adjust with salt and mix well. Serve in bowls.

Smoked Tofu Salad

If smoked tofu cannot be found, regular firm tofu can be used. Tofu will taste better if it is marinated for at least 2 hours before use.

INGREDIENTS:

8 oz of smoked tofu, cubed

12 dozen cherry tomatoes, sliced

MARINADE:

½ tsp salt

¼ tsp granulated sugar

3 tbsp sesame oil

1 tbsp rice vinegar

¾ tsp chili paste (optional)

Mix all marinade ingredients, then add tofu and tomatoes. This is best marinated for at least 1 hour in refrigerator before serving or can also be served immediately.

Pesto Pasta Salad

INGREDIENTS:

8 oz penne cooked al dente in salted water

1 cup pesto, store-bought

1 cup feta

1 cup ripe olives, chopped

¼ cup toasted pine nuts (optional)

¼ cup VOO

1 cup frozen mixed vegetables, thawed

6 cherry tomatoes, cut in half

salt and pepper to taste

Mix all ingredients with cooked pasta. Adjust with salt. Toss and refrigerate before serving.

Note: You can make your pesto at home or on board if you have a blender. Here is how: 2 bunches of basil, ½ cup of VOO, ¼ cup of pine nuts, and 3 garlic cloves. Pistachios can also be substituted. Wash basil and remove leaves from the stems. Place in blender, drizzle in some of the oil while blender is on. Add nuts and garlic. Continue to add oil while pureeing. If too dry, you may add more oil. Remove from processer, place in bowl and refrigerate.

Note: This can also be served as a main course.

Fish

Catch of the Day

This is a simple dish to prepare on any boat. I have done this many times, and my guests continue to marvel that this comes out of a galley.

INGREDIENTS:

1 lb of clams, washed

1 lb of mussels, washed and beard removed

1 lb prawns, peeled and deveined—tail removed

1 cup white wine

6 garlic cloves, minced

1 medium onion, chopped

2 sprigs of cilantro or parsley or both, roughly chopped

2 cup fish stock, reserved from cooking fish

½ cup VOO

1 tbsp sea salt

1 tbsp flour

salt and pepper to taste

sliced hard-crust bread

METHOD:

Place enough water in a pot to cover clams and mussels. Add onions and salt and cook till mussels open. About 10–12 minutes. Using a colander strain and reserve the juices as your fish stock. In the meantime, heat up the VOO and sauté the garlic. Add the flour to make rue. Add a cup of fish stock and the wine. If too thick, add more stock. Add prawns cook for 3 minutes then add shellfish and cook for another couple of minutes. To serve, place in a bowl and sprinkle with parsley to garnish. Serves 4–6. Prep time about 20 minutes.

Note: Fish can be pan fried, then pour sauce over fish.

Chickpea and Salmon Casserole

Sailing to Mexico from Vancouver, we had some awesome meals. I mean gourmet. It was like going out to eat every mealtime. This was easy because we stopped to provision along the way. We did not have to eat canned meals or food that had to be hydrated.

INGREDIENTS:

1 lb of smoked salmon or whole chunks of canned salmon

1 small can of cooked chickpeas (garbanzo beans)

1 medium onion, peeled and chopped

3 garlic cloves, minced

1 bunch of spinach, washed. Frozen spinach can also be used.
However, make sure it is well thawed and water is squeezed out.

½ cup VOO

sea salt

METHOD:

Sauté onion and garlic in oil. Add spinach and smoked salmon. Drain chickpeas and add contents to salmon and spinach mix. Add salt to taste. Divide into individual dishes and serve. If you have the time, this dish can be baked. To bake, beat 2 eggs, fold into salmon mix, grate Parmesan and sprinkle on top, and bake at 375° for 25 minutes or until set and cheese is melted.

Salmon in Chermoula
(BAKED SALMON IN GARLIC SAUCE)

This may sound fancy and gourmet and it is. You can eat gourmet on your boat. Tucked away in a small cove with your hook set with a slight breeze a slight swing now and then and a glass of your favorite wine, this dish can be on your table in 30 minutes. If this is the catch of the day, it makes it even better.

INGREDIENTS:

4 salmon steaks

3 ripe tomatoes

2 roasted red pepper sliced and store-bought

1 cup pitted ripe olives or kalamata olives, pitted

1 tsp ground cumin

¼ tsp hot pepper flakes

2 cloves of crushed garlic

1 tsp regular Hungarian paprika or smoked paprika

3 tbsp VOO

½ cup of water

1 tsp ground ginger

CHERMOULA SAUCE:

The sauce can be made before leaving home or, if you have a blender on hand, can be made on board or ingredients crushed in a bowl. Combine the last seven ingredients and blend. Marinate fish in sauce for at least 1 hour. Grease a baking dish and lay roasted red peppers in dish. Place marinated fish on peppers; pour marinade over fish. Cut tomatoes in half and line the sides of baking dish. Top fish with sliced olives, cover with tin foil, and bake for 25–30 minutes at 375°. Garnish with lemon wedges and parsley.

Note: The fish should be marinated in a ziplock bag at home and just baked aboard. Any fish can be used.

Prawn and Mussels Skewers on Plain Rice

INGREDIENTS:

1 lb 20–30 count peeled and deveined prawns with tail on

½ lb of shelled mussels

1 dozen cherry tomatoes

2 eggs beaten

1 cup flour

1 cup bread crumbs

cooking oil

salt and pepper

METHOD:

Cook mussels in salted boiling water for about 3–5 minutes. Drain water and let it cool. Remove mussels from shell. Drench in flour, then egg wash and finally in bread crumbs. Use the same procedure for the prawns. Skewer while alternating the prawns and mussels with cherry tomato. At this stage the skewers can be baked or grilled. Before skewering, the mussels and prawns can also be deep fried. Serve with tartar sauce or a sweet and sour sauce and on a bed of seasoned, plain rice or vegetables and green salad

Note: For seasoned rice, cook rice and add garlic, salt and pepper to taste, with some paprika and chopped cilantro.

Cataplan
(SEAFOOD STEW)

This dish was inspired by a trip I made to Portugal a few years ago. The Portuguese made this look so simple that I decided to try it on my boat. Simple and delicious is the only way to describe this. If you do any kind of boating in the cooler months of the year, this will warm not only your crew but your spirits. There are many ingredients in this dish, but it is worth it.

INGREDIENTS:

½ lb rice noodles

2 green peppers and 2 red peppers, cubed

1 green and 1 yellow zucchini, cubed to bite-size pieces

4 garlic cloves, chopped

1 large onion, sliced

3 tomatoes cut into wedges

1 cup white wine

1 cup fish or chicken stock

1 lb of salmon or any other firm fish

1 lb of large prawns

½ lb of mussels

½ cup of VOO

3 sprigs of cilantro or Italian parsley, chopped

juice of a lime and extra lime for garnishing

salt and pepper

some hard-crust bread

METHOD

Cook noodles in boiling salt water until al dente. Drain and save the water for cooking the fish. Sauté all veggies, onion, and garlic in oil. Add wine. Cook for another 2 minutes to reduce. Add stock and lime juice, heat just to boiling. Then add prawns, mussels, and salmon. Cook till mussels open. Mix in chopped cilantro and noodles then drizzle with VOO. Garnish with lime wedges and serve hot in a bowl with pieces of bread to soak up the juices.

Seafood over Pasta with Arugula

Another comfort food on the boat. This dish can be prepared on the way or when moored. Simply delicious.

INGREDIENTS:

½ lb linguine or spaghetti cooked al dente

3 cloves of garlic

½ red onion, chopped

1 shallot

¼ cup VOO

½ cup sun-dried tomatoes preferably in oil, minced

1 cup of white wine (Pinot Grigio)

1 lb. large prawns

½ lb clams or shelled mussels

arugula or any mixed greens

METHOD:

Cook pasta until al dente. Drain and set aside. In the meantime, sauté garlic, onions, shallots, and sun-dried tomatoes until onions are translucent. Add wine and cook for another 3 minutes. Add prawns and shellfish. When the mussels open or the shrimp turns pink, remove from heat. To serve, place arugula then pasta on top, and top with seafood and sauce.

Crusted Halibut

Halibut is a simple dish to prepare. Most people overcook it; hence, it ends up being tough as your hull and difficult to eat. Fresh halibut, especially if it is caught off your boat, is amazingly awesome. Follow these simple instructions, and you will have a great meal every time. There are many ways to prepare halibut, but frying it for fish and chips? Well. If you want a thick white fish for that, try mahi mahi, then you will think that you have die and gone to heaven.

INGREDIENTS:

2 lb halibut, cut into ¾- to 1-inch steaks, bone in

2 cups of ground pistachio nuts or your favorite nut (optional) or fine bread crumbs

1 cup of tequila or sweet white wine

2 eggs beaten

1 cup of flour

¼ cup VOO

salt and pepper to taste

juice of 2 limes or lemon

lime wedges for garnishing

METHOD:

Marinate the steaks in 2 tbsp of sea salt, tequila, lime juice, and olive oil for about an hour. This can be done before casting off in a ziplock freezer bag. To bake halibut, dip a steak in the egg wash, roll it in the ground nuts or bread crumbs, and set aside on baking pan. Continue till all the steaks are done. If you have saran wrap aboard, individually wrap each steak, or leave steaks on baking pan and refrigerate for ½ hour if it is possible. Remove steak from refrigerator, then remove saran wrap. Bake at 400° in the oven for 20 minutes. The thickness of the steak will determine the baking time. However, check for doneness. Garnish with lime wedges.

Note: Any white fish or salmon can be prepared using this method. Parchment paper in the baking dish will help prevent fish from sticking.

Note: Steaks can be panfried making sure that they do not burn.

The Fish Bowl

This dish was inspired by sheer imagination on my sailing trip from Tahiti to Honolulu. We finally caught some fish of which there was a good-looking mahi mahi. So as main dishwasher, butler, chef, and sailor, I had to create something different with this fish. After a while, fish dinners at sea become very boring. While I looked through the food storage bin, *aha*, I found a coconut and some dry stir-fry noodles. I know how to make coconut milk having grown up in the Caribbean. Today you can buy a can of coconut milk in your grocery store. Coconut is the magic ingredient.

INGREDIENTS:

2 lbs of mahimahi, cubed, or any other firm white fish. I have done this dish with salmon.

2 cans of coconut milk

1 medium onion

4 heads of garlic

½ cup white wine

3 carrots, sliced

8 florets of broccoli

6 mushrooms, sliced

1/2 lb. of dry stir-fry precooked noodles or any other fast-cooking noodles

VOO

12 fresh basil leaves (dry oregano or majoram)

METHOD:

In a deep pot, sauté onions and garlic in oil. When onions are translucent, add wine and reduce. Add both cans of coconut milk, carrots, and salt to taste. Cook for another 5 minutes. Add noodles and cook while stirring a few times until al dente. Add fish, all the basil and broccoli. Cook for 3 minutes and avoid stirring too much. Turn off heat and cover pot. Serve hot in a bowl.

Note: You can use any firm white fish.

Genoa Bay Mussels

You have traversed the beach after you set the hook and have found a bunch of mussels, It is time for a feast. Of course, you have white wine on the boat, right?

INGREDIENTS:

mussels, enough to feed your guest

3 heads of garlic, chopped

1 cup white wine

1 tsp of any dry spices on board

chicken broth or water

1 cup VOO

3 sprigs of parsley/cilantro, chopped

hard-crust bread to soak up juices

tomato sauce (optional)

Salt and pepper to taste

METHOD:

Sauté garlic in some of the VOO. Add wine, reduce, and add broth, salt and pepper to taste. If you use tomato sauce, add it at this stage. Add mussels, cover and simmer. Mix occasionally till mussels open. Serve in large bowls with sliced bread on the side. Pour some VOO over mussels and sprinkle with parsley.

Linguine Ala Proscuitto and Smoked Salmon

INGREDIENTS:

8 oz heavy cream

linguine

garlic

8 oz smoked salmon

1 oz prosciutto

8–12 oz butter squash

parsley

basil

PREP:

Cook linguine al dente with salt

Grill prosciutto lightly

Bake cubed squash al dente

SAUCE:

Sauté garlic

Add cream and prosciutto while stirring

Add wine, smoked salmon

Reduce to ½ volume and add salt and pepper to taste

Combine sauce with linguine, parsley, basil, and squash

Garnish with basil and green goddess sauce

Spaghetti with Mussels

INGREDIENTS:

12 ½ of spaghetti
2 lb cleaned mussels
1 green onion
2 garlic cloves
extra virgin oil
chili
parsley
basil
marjoram
½ glass of white wine

METHOD:

Clean mussels, and open on the half shell and leave in water to soak. Bring a large pot of salted water to a boil to cook spaghetti. Heat oil in a large pan and sauté garlic, chili, onion, and some of the other aromatic herbs. Pour the shelled mussels, the wine, and the mussel water in, making sure the water is strained to prevent sand from going into the sauce. Let the liquid absorb on a high flame for a few minutes, then add spaghetti and the rest of aromatic herbs. Transfer to serving dish and add extra virgin oil and salt and pepper to taste. Serve hot.

Meat

Meatballs over Spaghetti

Oh yes, comfort food for a fall or winter-boating day. Meatballs can be premade before casting off or made at anchor.

INGREDIENTS:

1 lb ground beef

1 lb of hot Italian sausage, casings removed

1 egg, beaten

1 cup of bread crumbs or 4 slices of stale bread soaked in milk

1 tsp sea salt

3 garlic cloves, chopped, or 1 tbsp ground garlic

1 lb of cherry tomatoes, sliced

½ bunch of parsley, chopped

For sauce:

1 bottle of your favorite tomato sauce, store-bought

METHOD:

Mix all ingredients and form balls the size of a medium egg. Place meatballs in a baking pan and bake at 375° for 20 minutes. Do not overcook as the meatballs will cook further in sauce. Drain off fat and place balls in a pot. Pour tomato sauce and tomatoes over meatballs and simmer for ½ hour over very low heat. Serve over spaghetti or your favorite pasta.

Note: Once the meat is mixed, this dish can be made into a meat loaf by placing in a loaf pan and baking.

Meat Loaf on a Boat

This dish is scrumptious comfort food any time of the year while boating, but more so in the fall, winter, and even spring. I prepare meat loaf in February while sailing around the gulf islands in Canada. It takes a little longer than normal, about 45 minutes from start to finish, but if you are prepared, the time can be shorter. Here we go.

INGREDIENTS:

1 ½ lb lean ground beef (chicken, lamb, or turkey can be substituted)

1 lb mild Italian sausage (chorizo)

1 medium onion, chopped

1 bunch of cilantro, chopped,

4 garlic cloves, minced

3 sprigs of green onions

2 stems of celery, finely chopped

1 tbsp each of oregano and marjoram

3 boiled eggs (optional)

12 green olives (optional)

1 cup bread crumbs, panko

2 eggs beaten

VOO

parchment paper (optional)

for the sauce:

1 ½ cup ketchup

½ cup Dijon mustard

METHOD:

Mix meats, chopped herbs, and dry herbs. Add beaten eggs and mix. Add panko and mix some more until all ingredients are combined. Make meat mixture into a big ball then shape into your baking dish.

If olives and boiled eggs are used, use your finger and form a depression on meat, place eggs on end, cover eggs with some meat, and repeat the same for olives.

For sauce, combine ketchup and mustard. Paint top of meat with sauce. Bake for 30 minutes at 400°. Slice and serve.

Note: The meat can be divided into 2 sections and baked in two 5 × 8 × 3 baking dishes.

Meat Loaf Sandwich

If you made meatloaf the night before, you gotta have a meat loaf sandwich the next day for lunch. Guess what, I have it for breakfast.

INGREDIENTS:

multigrain bread (toasted or untoasted)

mayo

Dijon mustard

tomato

lettuce (optional)

slices of raw onions

ketchup (optional)

METHOD:

Spread mayo over one slice of bread and mustard on the other. If ketchup is used, put it on the side with the mustard. Place sliced meat loaf, then tomato and sliced onions. Top with other slice of bread, cut into 2 triangles and serve.

Chicago~style Sausage and Pepper

I lived in Chicago for a number of years and Lake Michigan was my playground. Sailing across the lake was a lot of fun, and eating Chicago style while sailing was even more fun. Nothing is better than enjoying Italian sausage and peppers way out on the lake when the city of Chicago is just a glimpse in the distance lit by the setting sun.

INGREDIENTS:

2 lb of mild or hot Italian sausage

2 green peppers

2 red peppers

2 yellow peppers

2 tsp dry oregano

2 tsp dry marjoram

6 garlic cloves, chopped

2 medium onion, sliced

½ bunch Italian parsley

½ tbsp sea salt

VOO

METHOD:

Cook sausages in frying pan. Drain fat, cool, and slice at an angle in 1-inch pieces. In the meantime, sauté all the other ingredients in VOO except the parsley. Cook until onions are translucent, then add the sausage and a little water or wine if too dry and cook until heated through. Add the parsley, mix, and serve with hard-crust bread or by itself. Adjust with salt and pepper to taste

South Pacific Delight

This recipe was given to me by a seasoned sailor while sailing on the Pacific. He swore that you can use this as an appetizer or main course. He said that it has your cheese, meat, and veggies.

INGREDIENTS:

1 lb cooked sausage meat (ground beef, turkey, or chicken)

8 oz of cream cheese

12 oz can of diced tomato

½ jalapeño, finely chopped

½ tbsp salt

1 bag of chips

METHOD:

Mix all ingredients while cooked meat is still hot. Taste for salt and add if needed. Serve warm with chips.

Lamb Burgers

Good old burgers. Living on Salt Spring Island, lamb is a favourite. Try serving your friends lamb and they will love you for life. You can buy these in the supermarket, but it's best to make them yourself. Have them with a glass of your favourite wine. I love them with a dry red. Burgers can be made before casting off.

INGREDIENTS:

2 lb. of ground lamb

1 tbsp rosemary

1 tbsp of sea salt or less to your taste

1 tbsp of dry oregano

1 tbsp of dry thyme

1 egg beaten

1 cup bread crumbs

3 garlic cloves, minced, or 1 tbsp ground garlic

3 sprigs of parsley or cilantro, finely chopped

To serve: hamburger buns, tomato slices, mayo, ketchup, and mint jelly (optional

METHOD:

Mix all ingredients and form burgers about 3½ inches in diameter. Grill or panfry to your doneness. Serve on buns with Dijon mustard, tomato slices, and milt jelly.

Good Old Steak

If you do not have a grill on your boat, here is how to enjoy a steak. The number of steaks will depend on your guest count.

INGREDIENTS:

4 steaks of your choice

sea salt

VOO

3 cloves of garlic, minced

1 tbsp garlic powder for marinade

1 large onion, sliced

12 mushrooms, sliced

½ cup red or white wine

METHOD:

Marinate steaks in a ziplock bag with some of the oil, garlic, and salt for at least 1 hour. Grill steaks to doneness. To panfry, heat oil in a frying pan. When hot, place the steak in pan and cook for about 3 minutes. Flip the steak and cook other side for 3 minutes. The steak should be a medium rare. If required, the steak can be cooked longer. Remove the steak from the pan and let it rest. In the meantime, use the same pan for sautéing the mushrooms with minced garlic and onions. Add the wine, deglaze, and reduce to about half the volume. To serve, top steaks with mushroom mixture.

Breaded Lamb Chops

INGREDIENTS:

6 lamb chops about 6–8 oz each

2 eggs

2 cups fine bread crumbs

1 teaspoon garlic powder

1 teaspoon dry rosemary

1 teaspoon cumin powder

¼ cup salt for brine

parsley/cilantro for garnishing

METHOD:

Dissolve salt in 4 cups of water for brine and marinate chops overnight or for at least 1 hour. Mix all other ingredients except eggs and set aside. Beat eggs in a small bowl and set aside. Remove chops from marinade and pat dry. Dip chops in egg wash, roll and press in bread crumbs, then dip in egg wash again, and lastly, in bread crumb mix. Place in an oiled baking pan. Repeat until all chops are done. Bake at 375° until chops are done.

Serve with rice or couscous and veggies. Garnish with cilantro or parsley. Serves six.

Chicken

Mochiko Chicken

Well, you do not have to be in Hawaii to enjoy this awesome dish. This can be prepared by anyone who has never worked in a galley. Bring the ingredients aboard or marinate the chicken before you depart and that's it.

INGREDIENTS:

2 lb boneless chicken breast

2 tbsp white sugar

2 tsp sea salt

1 egg beaten

1 tbsp soy sauce

1 tsp garlic powder

1 tsp toasted sesame seed

1 cup flour

½ cup water

METHOD:

Mix all ingredients except chicken. If batter is too thick, add a little more water. Dip chicken in batter and bake at 400° on top rack of oven for 10 minutes. Turn oven down to 375° and continue to bake for another 20 minutes or until batter is brown. Serve on rice with green salad.

Wing on Wing
EASY WINGS RUB A DUB

Pretend you are in the Caribbean and the sun is shining down on you. The only thing missing is a rum and coke and some jerk. You've got it. Simple jerk wings. This recipe can also be used on other chicken parts or pork.

INGREDIENTS:
3 lbs of chicken wings
½ cup dry jerk mix rub (store-bought)
VOO

METHOD:

Rub chicken with oil. Pour all the jerk mix over the chicken and mix well. Let it marinate in fridge for at least 1 hour. Bake at 375° for at least 45 minutes or till done. Serve with rice and peas or plain rice and veggies. Pour leftover baking sauce over rice and veggies.

Pesto Chicken

INGREDIENTS:

2 lb boneless, skinless chicken breast

8 oz of pesto, store-bought or homemade

1 tbsp salt

1 tbsp olive oil to grease baking pan

METHOD:

If chicken is very thick, split in half. Sprinkle both sides with salt. Coat both sides of chicken breast with pesto and place in baking pan, greased with olive oil. Let it sit for ½ hour, then bake at 375° for 1 hour. Serve over risotto or couscous. Garnish with basil or Italian parsley.

Jerk Chicken

Ya man, you can experience the Jamaican jerk on your boat. Jamaica is known for its jerk pork. In the western world, though, most people use this special spice on chicken. On your boat it is better to purchase the jerk rub, which can be in a liquid form or a dry rub. Careful not to use too much as it may be spicy. Also do not add any salt to meat, fish, or chicken. The spice is already salty.

INGREDIENTS:

enough jerk spice (store-bought) to rub chicken

2 lb chicken legs and thighs separated.

½ cup cooking oil

METHOD:

Coat chicken with oil, then rub chicken pieces with jerk mix and marinate for at least 1 hour, or even better overnight. Bake uncovered at 400° for 40 minutes or until chicken is done. The chicken can also be grilled

Honey Chicken

When boat is home, *yes*, honey I'm home. This is a welcoming chicken dish anytime whether you live aboard or are just out for fun with friends and family.

INGREDIENTS:

1 whole chicken cut into pieces or 2 lb chicken breast

2 tbsp honey mustard

1 tbsp Dijon mustard

3 garlic cloves, finely chopped

1 medium onion, sliced

1 cup of green tea

½ tbsp sea salt

2 tbsp balsamic vinegar

METHOD:

Mix all ingredients and marinate chicken for at least 1 hour. Better to marinate overnight in a ziplock bag placed in the refrigerator. Remove chicken from marinade and place in a baking dish or Dutch oven. Bake at 400° for 45 minutes to 1 hour. Turn chicken pieces over once while baking. Serve with baked or mashed potato.

Toto Santos Chicken Breast

this is a surprinsingly easy dish to make on a boat. Actually, the first time I tried it was while boating, I was amazed how simple it was.

INGREDIENTS:

1 large jar of salsa

¼ cup of lime juice

1 bunch of cilantro, chopped

1 cup Mexican or other cheese

3 chicken breasts

6 tortillas

Salt to taste

METHOD:

Marinate chicken in first 3 ingredients overnight or for a few hours. Bake or grill chicken. Let it cool, then shred chicken. Place shredded chicken in marinade, add cilantro and sauté for 3 minutes. In the meantime, heat tortillas. Fill tortillas with chicken mix, add cheese and fold. Serve hot with a salad.

Taquitos with Leftover Chicken

INGREDIENTS:

VOO

1 medium onion, minced

3 garlic cloves, minced

1 tsp paprika

1 tsp cumin

sea salt

1 bunch cilantro, chopped

2 cups shredded chicken

6 or 8 inch flour tortillas

1 cup cheese (cheddar or queso fresco)

METHOD:

Sauté onions and garlic in VOO. Add paprika, cumin and cook for another 2 minutes. Add shredded chicken and cilantro. Turn off heat, add cilantro and salt and pepper to taste. Fold cheese into mixture. Spoon enough into tortillas and fold. Serve hot.

Anchor Chicken Bake

As the name suggest, this dish is better prepared when you are on the hook after a long day of boating. Sit back, relax, pour yourself a glass of wine, or have a beer. You can prepare this dish in 5 minutes and let the oven do the rest.

INGREDIENTS:

6 boneless, skinless chicken thighs or 2 medium breast, skinless and cut into 4 pieces

1 can of your favorite chunky tomato sauce

2 tablespoon of dry oregano, marjoram, and thyme

½ glass wine or whatever you are drinking—even beer is good

4 medium carrots cut into ½ pieces

2 large potatoes, cubed

salt and pepper

METHOD:

Heat oven up to 400°. Sprinkle chicken with dry spices, salt, and pepper. Place chopped carrots and potato in the baking dish. Top the veggies with the chicken, and pour the wine over chicken, then top with the whole can of tomato sauce. Do not mix. Cover baking dish or use tinfoil if there is no lid. Bake in oven for about 30 minutes or until chicken is done.

Note: Chicken thighs will take longer to cook.

Easter, Thanksgiving, and Christmas Turkey

Yup, that's right. These holidays can be celebrated on your boat without all the fuss. You can serve turkey for the holidays by baking it in your minioven. Make sure you have all ingredients before you cast off.

METHOD:

Heat oven to 400°. Mix both mustards and rub skin side of turkey breast. Season with salt and pepper and place in baking bag. When the oven reaches temperature, place turkey in oven and bake for about 1 hour or longer, depending the size of the breast. Remove from oven, cool and serve. In the meantime, prepare the stuffing by sautéing remaining ingredients in VOO, except the bread, until they are done for about 12 minutes. Add the bread and the wine. Mix well. If too dry, add a cup of water. The bread will soak up the fluids, but it should be moist. When all is incorporated, place mixture in a baking dish and bake with the turkey for the last 30 minutes. Remove from oven, cool and serve.

INGREDIENTS:

fresh turkey breast

6 slices of white several days old bread or 6 cups bread cubes

2 celery stalks, chopped

1 bunch of green onions, roughly chopped

4 garlic cloves, minced

2 medium onions, chopped

1 cup dry cranberries (optional)

1 cup dry mushrooms, soaked in water, or 2 cup mushrooms, sliced

1 tbsp sea salt

1 tsp ground fresh pepper

1 cup white wine

1 turkey bag for baking

¼ cup Dijon mustard

2 tbsp dry mustard

Finger~Licking BBQ Chicken

This is part of a typical summer boating menu. Regardless of where you are boating, this dish comes in handy because it is simple and appetizing.

INGREDIENTS:

2 lb of chicken parts or breast

12 oz of BBQ sauce, store-bought

salt

2 tbsp garlic powder

2 tbsp onion powder

2 tbsp dry thyme or oregano

1 tsp cayenne pepper

½ cup dark or white rum

1 cup red wine (optional)

METHOD:

Mix all the ingredients in a bowl large enough to hold the chicken. Add the chicken and marinate in a ziplock bag for at least 1 hour, preferably overnight. Remove the chicken from the bag, shake off excess sauce, and grill over a medium heat. Baste occasionally with sauce. After grilling, bring the leftover sauce to a boil and pour over the chicken. To bake, place the chicken with sauce in a baking pan. Do not cover and place in a 400° oven for 45 minutes or until chicken is done and the sauce is reduced to less than ½.

Pasta

Penne with Tequila Prawns

Fast and satisfying dinner anytime while boating. Even for those who do not like cooking. Linguine can also be substituted for penne.

INGREDIENTS:

8 oz of penne

½ cup VOO

4 garlic cloves, minced

1 lb of large prawns (16–30 count)

1 cups of cream

1 cup white wine

1 tbsp sea salt

1 tbsp dry oregano

2 sprigs of basil, roughly chopped

METHOD:

Marinate shrimp with tequila, salt, oregano, and some olive oil. Cook pasta al dente, drain and set aside. Pour remainder of olive oil in a frying pan under medium heat and sauté garlic. Add wine and continue to cook for 2 minutes. Add cream slowly while stirring, careful not to boil. Add shrimp and cook for 3 minutes. Turn heat down, add pasta and mix. When all the fluid is combined with pasta, turn heat off. Sprinkle with basil and serve hot in a bowl or deep plate.

Linguine with Clams in White Sauce

Another 30 minute boat classic. If you happen to catch the clams right off your boat that day, clean well and use this method to prepare your dish.

INGREDIENTS:

10–12 oz of linguine, cooked al dente

2–3 tbsp of unsalted butter

1 medium onion, thinly sliced

2 garlic cloves, minced

½ cup white wine

½ cup VOO

salt and pepper

1 can of clam sauce (13 oz)

2 cans of clams, store-bought. Retain juice after opening.

4 sprigs parsley, chopped

1 cup shaved Parmesan cheese

METHOD:

Sauté onions and garlic in butter and 2 tbsp of the VOO. Add the wine and reduce by ¼. Add the clam sauce and heat for another 2 minutes. Add the clams and continue to cook for another 3 minutes. Add half of the cheese and all other ingredients and mix well. Adjust for salt. If too dry, add some of the reserved clam juice or a tablespoon of water at a time. Serve with the other half of the grated Parmesan in a bowl for topping.

Note: 1 dozen fresh clams, shell remove and cleaned can be used.

T and T ~ Tortellini with Tuna

INGREDIENTS:

16 oz of frozen tortellini, cooked al dente

1 cup frozen mixed veggies

1 cup diced red pepper

2 cans, 10 oz of canned tuna or smoked salmon

2 garlic cloves

parsley

juice of ½ a lemon

VOO

METHOD:

Thaw out frozen veggies in hot water. Add to tortellini. Sauté garlic and pepper in VOO. Add tortellini, tuna and lemon juice. Now add this to tortellini mix. Add parsley. Mix well and serve.

Vegetarian Spaghetti with Spinach, Lentils, and Chard

Fragrant vegetarian dish with protein. This is as easy as 1-2-3. You cook the lentils, the pasta, and the chard, mix, and you are done.

INGREDIENTS:

1½ cups of lentils (or any other beans)

2 stalks of celery, chopped in ½ inch pieces

8 oz of spaghetti

3 heads of garlic, chopped

onion, chopped

cilantro, roughly chopped

2 heads of chard, cleaned, washed, and chopped. Use the white part of the chard stem.

VOO

salt and pepper

your favorite spices

METHOD:

Add 2½ cups of water to a pot, add the lentils and celery, 1 tbsp salt and a drizzle of oil. Cover and bring to a boil. Reduce the heat and cook until lentils absorb all the water and are al dente. If more water is needed before lentils are cooked, add a little at a time. Remove from heat. In the meantime, boil salted water in another pot and cook spaghetti al dente. When pasta is cooked, drain, drizzle with some VOO, mix, and set aside.

Sauté onion and garlic in oil and any spices you like; add chard and cook for another 5 minutes under low heat.

Mix pasta, chard, cilantro, and lentils. Adjust with salt and pepper, then serve. This dish can be eaten at room temperature or cold. Garnish with cilantro.

Sandwiches, Soups and Breakfast

Tuna Melt

Sandwiches are always fast, easy lunches on your first day out when you are shaking out the canvass.

INGREDIENTS:

2 cans of chunk tuna

1 medium shallot, minced

1 tbsp of lemon juice

salt and pepper

2 tomatoes, sliced

½ bunch parsley

sliced cheddar, medium or sharp

whole wheat bread

METHOD:

In a bowl, mix all ingredients except cheese, tomatoes, and bread. Spread mixture on one slice of bread and top with 2 tomato slices and cheese. Repeat for more sandwiches. Place under broiler till cheese is melted. Remove and top with other slice of bread.

Note: Chicken or salmon can be substituted for tuna and sandwiches can be grilled.

Grilled Cheese

This is another comfort food, especially if some of your guests are children; you are bound to make them happy.

INGREDIENTS FOR 1 SANDWICH:

2 slices of multigrain bread

aged cheddar

Gorgonzola

1 tsp oregano or marjoram

enough butter for 2 sides of bread

enough roasted red pepper for 1 side of the bread

sliced onions (optional)

VOO

METHOD:

Butter one side of each slice of bread. On one slice lay down Gorgonzola and cheddar, and on the other slice, unbuttered side, roasted pepper and sliced onions. In the meantime, heat up frying pan with a drizzle of oil. When pan is hot, reduce heat and place both slices of bread, butter side down, in frying pan and cover so cheese can melt about 3 minutes. Check to make sure that bread does not burn. Remove from pan once cheese is melted, slice and serve.

Note: Alternatively, the bread can be toasted; the preparation is the same, but instead of pan grilling, the bread can be placed under the broiler.

BLT

This is not your normal BLT. This version has the Caribbean twist. It will make your cheeks pucker and your taste buds wonder what happened.

INGREDIENTS FOR 1 SANDWICH:

2 slices of multigrain bread

½ of a ripe avocado

4 slices of bacon cooked not to crisp

½ tsp horseradish

1 lettuce leaf

1 tomato, sliced horizontally

juice of ½ of a lime

enough mayo for 2 slices of bread

1 tbsp VOO

METHOD:

Toast bread. Cut avocado in 1-inch strips and peel. Flatten pieces on a plate. Spread horseradish on one side of the bread slices. Spread avocado on top of the horseradish. Sprinkle avocado with lime juice. On the other slice of bread spread mayonnaise and top with bacon, lettuce, and tomato in that order. Drizzle with olive oil. Cover with other bread slice, cut in half, and serve.

Corn Muffin

Baking on a boat is difficult in the best of times. However, there is nothing better than having fresh baked muffins while boating to go with a nice brewed coffee.

INGREDIENTS:

2 packages corn muffin mix

1 can creamed corn

¼ cup honey

2 eggs

⅔ cup milk.

METHOD:

Heat oven at 350°. In the meantime, mix all ingredients very well. Pour mixture in muffin tins and bake for 20 minutes. Remove from oven and cool. Serve with butter.

Cowichan Bay Breakfast Casserole

Nestled in a beautiful bay on Vancouver Island on a bright, sunny day, I woke up with the urge to have bacon and eggs for breakfast, I went to the dock store and found bacon, eggs, and some cream. If you are unable to get cream, use milk if it is available or nothing at all. You can serve in about 30 minutes.

INGREDIENTS:

4 slices of bacon

2 slices of white day old bread. Cut into ½-inch pieces

¼ cup cream

6 eggs

pinch of salt and pepper

½ cup shredded Parmesan or aged cheddar

½ red pepper, diced (optional)

½ medium onion, chopped

green onions (scallions are optional)

nonstick skillet or cast iron frying pan

METHOD:

Cook bacon in skillet until crisp. Transfer bacon to paper towels to drain off excess fat. Pour off the fat except about 1 tbsp from skillet. Cook bread in skillet till brown. You may have to cook bread in 2 portions and, in that case, add some more oil. Sauté peppers and onion till onion is translucent. In the meantime, mix eggs, cream, salt, and pepper. Add crumbled bacon, cheese, and green onions. Add mixture to skillet and cook over medium heat, scraping bottom to make sure it does not stick to skillet. When eggs begin to set, fold in bread pieces. Place in oven and bake until golden. If you do not have an oven, once the egg is set, slide onto a plate, then slide back into the skillet with other side down. Serve.

Soup from the Sea of Cortez
(TORTILLA SOUP)

I made this soup on my way to Mexico. Making soup on a boat can be very challenging. Yet this is not difficult, but rather easy. It is easier to attempt this while tied up or on the hook. I have made soup while on the way, but please do not attempt this as a spill could be dangerous. You will enjoy this soup with a touch from south of the border.

INGREDIENTS:

1 large can of diced tomato 28 oz

1 can of coconut milk (optional)

4 cups of chicken broth

1 medium onion, chopped

4 sprigs of cilantro

¼ cup of wine, white or red or tequila

1 avocado sliced (optional)

plain yogurt or sour cream (optional)

grated cheese (optional)

salt and pepper

juice of 1 lime

tortilla chips

METHOD:

Sauté onions until translucent. Add wine and cook for another 3 minutes. Add diced tomato, chicken broth, coconut milk, and cook for 5 minutes. Turn down heat to low and simmer. At this stage, add salt and pepper to taste and lime juice. Stir and continue to simmer for 5 more minutes. Turn off heat and serve by pouring soup into bowl and top with cilantro, tortilla chips, avocado, and sour cream or yogurt. Delish, fast, and easy.

Nanoose Bay Drunken Prawn Taco

This is the ultimate fish shrip taco. The quickest dinner on your boat that's not only fast but healthy.

INGREDIENTS:

24 prawns, peeled and deveined

6 cloves of garlic, finely chopped

2 scallions, finely chopped

2 jalapeño peppers, seeded and finely chopped

VOO

½ cup tequila

2 sprigs of cilantro, chopped(optional)

zest of a small orange

zest of 1 lemon and juice from lemon

1 avocado, cut into thin slices

some store-bought salsa

six 6"–8" tortillas wrapped in a moist cloth and kept warm in the oven.

Tortillas can also be warmed up in frying pan.

METHOD:

Bring VOO to medium high on stove top, then add scallions, jalapeño and garlic. Sauté for 2 minutes. Turn up heat and add prawns. Stir then add tequila. Cook for 3–4 minutes or till prawns are done (pink). Add zest, cilantro, and lemon juice. Stir vigorously, remove from heat. To build the taco, add 4 shrimps to a tortilla, a slice of avocado, and 1 tablespoon each of raw onion and salsa. Fold and serve.

Note: Any white fish can be used. Grilled red snapper or mahimahi is great.

Scram and Mushrooms

Start the day with a simply filling breakfast which will hold you until lunch. On my trip from Tahiti to Hawaii, I found that the crew was happy with this dish, and lunch could be much later. Remember that a crew with a full stomach is a happy crew. Besides, this is so simple it can be prepared in any weather conditions as long as you have the ingredients.

INGREDIENTS:

8 oz mushrooms

8 eggs medium, cracked and beaten

2 green onions, chopped into ¼-inch pieces

1 medium red pepper seeds removed and thinly sliced

½ medium onion, chopped

¼ cup heavy cream (optional)

¼ cup regular cooking oil

salt and white pepper (black pepper can be used)

3 sprigs of parsley, chopped. Leave some for garnishing (optional).

1 tsp dry oregano or marjoram

julienned a med red pepper

METHOD:

Sauté onions and mushrooms on medium heat until onions are translucent about 5 minutes. Add all other ingredients except white pepper. Stir in eggs and cream. Keep stirring until eggs are set. Season with salt and pepper to taste. Serve individually or on large platter.

Sides, Pasta and Veggies

Unconventional Pizza

Pizza dough is easy to take along on a boating trip. You can also use pita bread for individual pizzas.

INGREDIENTS:

2 (8"–10") pizza dough

VOO

2 tomatoes sliced

12 fresh basil leaves, roughly chopped

2 cups mozzarella cheese

1 cup olive, chopped

½ dozen mushrooms, sliced

1 medium onion, sliced

4 garlic cloves, minced

2 cups tomato sauce with a pinch of salt and 2 tablespoon oregano mixed

And any leftover chicken or veggies (optional)

METHOD:

Drizzle VOO over the dough then, using a spoon, spread tomato sauce over bread. Spread mushrooms, onions, olives, tomatoes, and anything else you wish, then top with basil, garlic, and cheese. Bake at 450° for about 15 minutes or until cheese melts.

Mac and Cheese

Homemade with a taste second to none. This can be made at home and taken aboard serve hot or sea temperature.

METHOD:

Cook macaroni al dente, drain and set aside. Sauté onions, garlic, and oregano in VOO. Once onions are translucent, add cream and sauté for another 3 minutes. Turn heat off and add the macaroni, all the cheese except the Parmesan, and mix thoroughly. If it is too dry, add some more cream. Mixture should be moist. Taste for salt at this stage and adjust if necessary. Place mixture in baking pan, sprinkle with parsley and Parmesan, and place in a 375° oven for ¾ hour or until top is brown. Remove from oven, let it cool, then serve with a green salad.

Note: This dish can be pre-prepared at home or before boating and finished by baking on the boat.

INGREDIENTS:

1 lb of elbow macaroni cooked al dente

1 medium onion, chopped

2 garlic cloves, minced (2 tsp ground garlic powder)

2 cups aged yellow cheddar cheese

2 cups medium white cheddar

2 cups heavy cream

2 cups light cottage cheese

1 cup Parmesan

½ cup VOO

1 tbsp oregano

3 sprigs of parsley, chopped

salt and pepper to taste

INDEX*

Edwards Brothers, Inc.
Thorofare, NJ USA
March 28, 2012